You Think This Is
Funny, Miss Nurse?

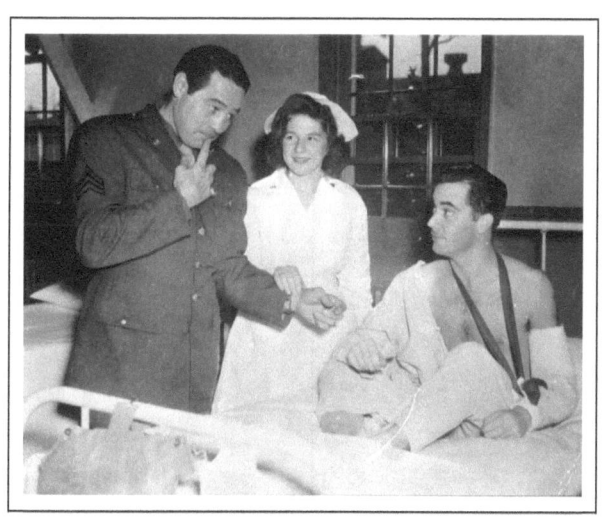

You Think This Is Funny, Miss Nurse?

JOE TEEPLES

authorHOUSE®

AuthorHouse™
1663 Liberty Drive
Bloomington, IN 47403
www.authorhouse.com
Phone: 1-800-839-8640

Model: Marie-Claude Samson
Photography by: Thomas Foose

Published by AuthorHouse   10/24/2014

ISBN: 978-1-4918-6866-9 (sc)
ISBN: 978-1-4918-6879-9 (e)

Library of Congress Control Number: 2014903762

This book is printed on acid-free paper.

It's A Crazy Profession.
But Remember...
These symptoms could get you
placed in a Sanitarium in 1865!

- Imaginary Female Trouble
- Women Trouble
- Female Disease
- Seduction and Disappointment
- Novel Reading

- Superstition
- Over Study of Religion
- Religious Enthusiasm
- Mental Excitement
- Bad Habits and Political Excitement
- Over Taxing Mental Powers
- Domestic Trouble

- Hysteria
- Immoral Life
- Greediness
- Egotism
- Laziness
- Hereditary Predisposition
- Marriage of son
- Asthma

- Nymphomania
- Masturbation for 30 years
- Masturbation and syphilis
- Tobacco and Masturbation
- Deranged Masturbation
- Suppressed Masturbation
- Excessive Sexual Abuse
- Self Abuse

You've Come a Long Way Since These 1887 Rules For Nurses!

- Nurses are to dust the patients' window sills and furniture daily.
- Ward floors will be swept and mopped each morning.
- Nurses are to bring in a scuttle of coal early in the morning to maintain an even temperature for the days business.
- Weekly, Nurses are to wash the windows to enhance the light. This is important for the patients' condition. The chimney must also be cleaned on a weekly basis.
- Trim wicks on kerosene lamps and ensure that they are filled weekly.
- Keep accurate and readable Nurses notes. Make your pens very carefully. Nurses are allowed to whittle the nibs to suit their individual preferences.

- Nurses will report not later than 7:00am and are expected to remain on the ward until 8:00pm every day.
- On the Sabbath, Nurses are excused from noon until 2:00pm.
- Graduate Nurses may be given one evening off for courting purposes if they are in good standing with the Director of Nurses. The Director may authorize two evenings off a week if the Nurse attends church on a regular basis.
- The use of tobacco or liquor by any Nurse, frequenting Dance Halls or a beauty shop will result in the Director of Nurses doubting the worth of the Nurse, her integrity and intentions.
- Nurses are expected to set aside a tidy sum of her daily earnings to provide for her benefits in her declining years. Nurses are not expected to become a burden on Society. It is recommended that if a Nurse earns $30 per month, $15 of that should be set aside.
- Any Nurse who serves her patients and doctors without fault and performs her labors faithfully for five years will be given an increase in pay of five cents per day. This is with the understanding that she has not outstanding hospital debts.

Get to know your fellow nursing students. They may be from small town America if:

- They have a rag for a gas cap
- They bought a TIVO because wrestling comes on while you're at work
- Their brother in law is also your uncle
- After making love, they ask their date to roll down the window

- They have more than three shirts with cut off sleeves
- They consider a six-pack of beer and a bug zapper quality entertainment
- They don't use rest stops if there is an empty milk jug in the car
- Their cars basic color is Bondo-gray

- Their life-time goal is to own a fireworks stand
- Their house doesn't have curtains but your truck does
- Their father wants them to quit school because of an opening at Quick Lube
- They still have an eight-track player

- Their front porch collapses and more than three dogs are killed
- They think a Volvo is part of a woman's anatomy
- They own a belt buckle that weighs more than three pounds
- They proudly display a gift purchased at Graceland

- They enjoy barbecue parties that feature Spam
- They were fired from your logging job because of their appearance
- Their dog and their wallet are both on chains
- They attend a funeral and there are more pick-up trucks than cars

- Their idea of safe sex is a padded head-board
- Their dad walks you to school because you are in the same grade
- Their dog can't watch them eat without gagging
- They think BMW is the call letters of the local radio station
- Their idea of a PDA is an ink pen and their palm
- Their spouse has a beer belly . . . . and they think its attractive
- They own more cowboy boots than sneakers
- Their idea of going out is boiler-makers at the wolf river tavern
- They own a copy of the video "Cannon Ball Run"
- They can relate to any of these items after reading this!

Study Guide for
Nursing Final Exam NRS 261

Instructions: Read each question carefully. Answer all questions within the 37 minute time limit.

History
Be prepared to discuss the Nursing Profession from the time of the Ancient Greeks to current day. Specifically address how the burning of Rome inspired the development of the modern Autoclave and how the Civil War lead to English as a common language among Nurses in America.

General Medicine
There is a shoebox beneath your seat. Inside you will find a steri-pen, gauze, a razor blade and a bottle of Jim Beam. Remove any organ from the person sitting to your left. Do not suture until the work has been approved by the test proctor.

Anatomy
Describe how Nursing helps you to fulfill your wildest desires. Be specific on how you found your G-Spot.

Biology
Create any carbon based life form using only the material found in any of the lunch boxes in the back room. Explain how your new creature could be a boon to mankind, or at least how it would amaze the Doctors.

Public Speaking
Develop a ten minute speech that would result in the soothing of a dozen or so zombies who are, at this time, approaching the classroom. Refrain from repeating the word 'brains' . . .

Management Science	Create an algorithm that will optimize the Nurse schedule for three shifts while keeping the entire ward happy and motivated. Explain how this algorithm will be dismissed by the Director of Nurses as being too practical.
Psychology	Explain the similarities among the minds of Ghost Hunters, Ancient Alien Theorists, Bigfoot Researchers and whoever is making the work schedule.
Sociology	Explain how merging cultures and societies tend to destroy one another. Construct an experiment to test your explanation, using the Doctors and Nurses on the Third Floor.
Economics	Using the concept of Supply and Demand, determine the maximum use for the homeless population.
Political Science	Using your parents money, start a business that will support the Republican Party in general, and Mitt Romney in particular. You may live in a friends basement while doing so.
Engineering	Fix the microwave in the Nurses Lunch Room.

Studying to pass the Nursing Boards can drive you insane!
(Model: Kendra Dicks)

The Nurses Horror scope

This explains all the strange stuff that happens to nurses!

Aquarius Jan 20-Feb 18

You are progressive with a creative and inventive mind. This causes you to lie a great deal, while being impractical. You tend to repeat mistakes and urinate frequently.

Pisces Feb 19-Mar 20

Your overactive imagination causes you to believe in any conspiracy theory that comes along. You are bold in social settings but cowardly in the workplace. This allows doctors to take sexual advantages of you when they sense that you are flaunting your imagined authority. You are best working alone at night, which makes you a perfect night shift employee.

Aries Mar 21-Apr 19

You are the sturdy pioneer type. You hold most of your co-workers in contempt and tend to think that you are better than the lot of them. When placed in a stressful situation you usually start a fire in the rest room and blame it on housekeeping.

Taurus Apr 20-May 20

You have a dogged determination that allows you to push square pegs into round holes easily. Practical and persistent, most of your co-workers just thing that you are bull-headed. This does not bother you, since most of them are jerks, anyway.

Gemini May 21-Jun 22

Your 'twins' are your greatest asset. The fact that you are bi-sexual makes you doubly popular at social events. A quick thinker, you can size up the situation rapidly and this has kept you from being involved in most of the degrading sexual parties that the Doctors invite you to. You really like the next person who walks into the room, but are hesitant to pursue a relationship with that person.

Cancer Jun 21-Jul 22

You are very understanding of other peoples problems. While you are sympathetic to a fault, you are also a sucker, always putting your job second while you volunteer to do everyone else's work. You will end up working for a hospice program in Miami . . .

Leo Jul 23-Aug 22

You consider yourself to be highly intelligent and a leader in your field. You couldn't be farther from the truth. Your short sighted efforts to improve the workplace usually result in chaos. Your co-workers see you as pushy... leaning towards being a bully. You tend to be an arrogant bastard.

Virgo Aug 23-Sep 22

You like everything in its place, put away properly. You tend to be a nit picking unemotional jerk who has been known to fall asleep during love making. This is fine with you, since you still think of yourself as a virgin. Your friends laugh behind your back at the 'born again virgin'.

Libra Sep 23-Oct 22

You enjoy the arts and love watching the musicians play, sing and dance. People think you may be gay, but you don't care. Most Libra men are pimps and most Libra women are closet lesbians. This causes you to change jobs frequently, but always in a venue with lots of beds, either a hotel, shelter or hospital.

Scorpio Oct 23-Nov 21

You are a shrewd business person who can create wealth at the drop of a hat. This is because you have no ethics. Your accumulation of wealth is a secret kept from your best friends and co-workers as you ride public transportation to and from work. The diapers that you put on your children were all hand me downs from your grandparents who taught you not to squander anything. Even paper diapers.

Sagittarius Nov 22 l-Dec 21

You are the most enthusiastic person in your group. This optimistic attitude and bubbly personality drive the rest of the workers on night shift to despise you. The fact that you have no real talent is hidden by your drive to drink heavily. At social events you are the life of the party . . . until you pass out.

Capricorn Dec 22-Jan 19

You are risk averse and very conservative. This means that you don't do much, don't accomplish much, and are generally just a lazy person. Capricorns never amount to much. When you spend time down town, the pigeons tend to mistake you for a statue . . . .

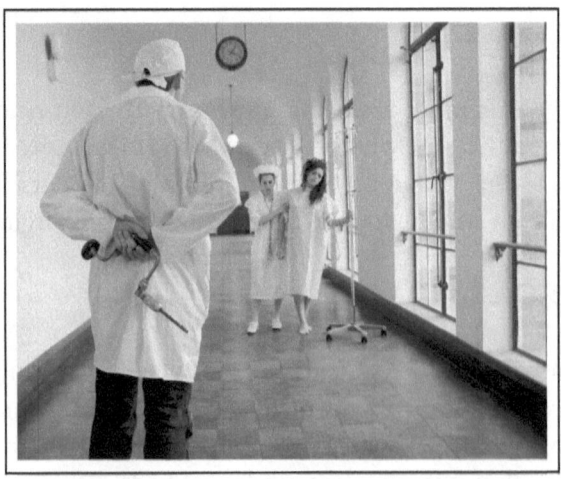

Sometimes Nursing is its own reward...

Nurses Sex Quiz

Circle the Best Choice

1. True   False   A clitoris is a type of flower

2. True   False   A pubic hair is a wild rabbit

3. True   False   A vulva is an automobile from Sweden

4. True   False   "Spread Eagle" is an extinct bird

5. True   False   The fallopian tube is part of a TV set

6. True   False   "Vagina" describes heart trouble

7. True   False   Copulation is sex between consenting policemen

8. True   False   McDonalds Golden Arches is a phallus symbol

9. True   False   A menstrual cycle has three wheels

10. True   False   It is dangerous to have a wet dream under an electric blanket

11. True   False   Fellatio is an Italian dagger

12. True   False   A G-String is a weapon used by G-men in the 1950's

13. True   False   Semen is a term for sailors in the Persian Gulf

14. True   False   An anus is a Latin word describing a period of time

15. True   False   Testicles are found on an octopus

16. True   False   Cunnilingus is a person who can speak three languages

17. True   False   Asphalt is a term used to describe rectal problems

18. True   False   Kotex is a radio station in Fort Worth, Texas

19. True   False   Masturbate is used by experts to catch large fish

20. True   False   Coitus is a musical instrument

21. True   False   Fetus is a character on Gunsmoke

22. True   False   An umbilical cord is part of a parachute

23. True False A condom is an apartment complex

24. True False A rectum is what you are for taking this test

25. True False Peter Pan is a wash basin in a house of ill repute

Extra Credit:

True False Oral sex is a faith healer from Oklahoma

True False Ping Pong Balls is a Chinese venereal disease

True False Free floating anxiety is an astronauts phobic fear of weightlessness

During Nursing classes you will be repeatedly
reminded to take Safety seriously . . .
(Model: Lindsay McCoy)

Nursing School

People enter the nursing profession for a variety of reasons. Here are a few of the reasons that people become nurses:

- Sexy white uniforms or comfy scrubs with fashionable shoes
- Outstanding pay and flexible hours
- Handsome, intelligent, young doctors as seen on TV
- Doctors who give clear orders and have impeccable handwriting.
- Be on the giving end of a needle for a change.
- The opportunity to see rare and exciting diseases up close.
- The knowledge that all bleeding stops . . . eventually.
- Interesting sounds and aromas.
- Enough charting to navigate around the world.
- Holidays with all your friends . . . . At work, of course.
- Knowing that most patients survive no matter what you do to them

Ode to a Mammogram

For years and years they told me,
"Be careful of your breasts,
Don't ever squeeze or bruise them,
And give them monthly tests."

So I heeded all their warnings
And protected them by law.
Guarded them very carefully
And always wore a bra.

After 30 years of careful care
The doctor found a lump.
He ordered up a mammogram
To look inside that clump.

"Stand very close," she said As
she got my tit in line. "Tell me
if it hurts," she said
"Ah yes, there, that's just fine."

She stepped upon a pedal I
could not believe my eyes!
A plastic plate was pressing down . . . .
My boob was in a vice!!!!

My skin was stretched and stretched
From way up by my chin.
My poor tit was being squashed
To Swedish pancake thin!

Excruciating pain I felt
Within it's vice-like grip.
A prisoner in this vicious thing
My poor defenseless tit!!!!

"Take a deep breath," she said
to me. Who does she think she's
kidding? My chest is smashed in
her machine, Can't breathe and
woozy I'm getting!

"There, that was good," I heard her say
As the room was slowly swaying.
"Now, let's do the other one."
Lord have mercy, I was praying!

It squeezed me up and
down. It squeezed from
side to side.
I'll bet SHE never had this done
To HER tender little hide!!!

If I had no problem when I came
in, I surely had one now . . . .
If there had been a cyst in there
It would have popped—KER POW!!!!!

This machine must have been made by
man, Of this I have no doubt.
I'd like to get his balls in
there. For month's he'd do without!!!!!!!

Now that you're experienced . . . .

**You may join the management team as they
strive to fill the Head Nurse Position!**

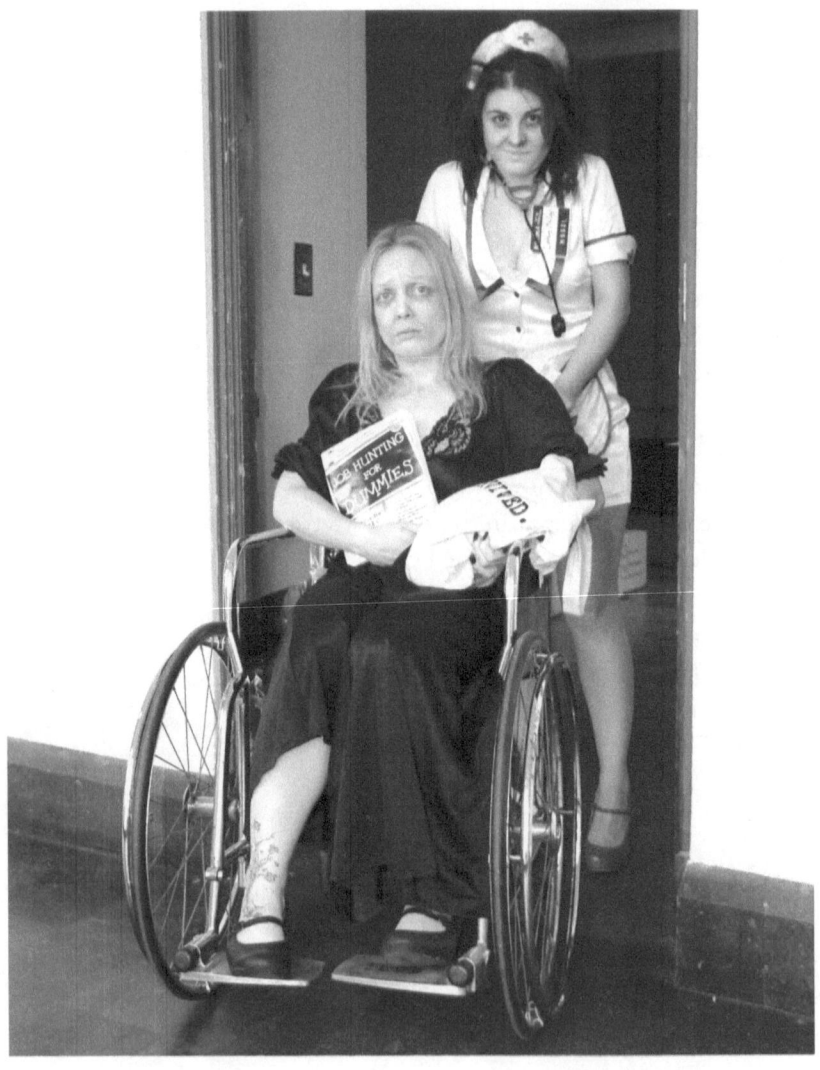

The College Head of the Nursing Department will
do everything she can to help you find a job . . .
(Model: Lindsay McCoy, Kendra Dicks)

Change to Nurses Policy and Procedures Manual

Subject: Permissible phrases for performance evaluations

In an effort to increase efficiency for this hospital we are adopting a system of performance evaluation wherein supervisors merely pick and choose from various phrases to complete the performance appraisal and the secretarial staff will fill in the report for signature.

This new format will provide for continuity among various wards and will significantly reduce errors, while at the same time increasing the time that nurses have available to dedicate to bedside treatment.

Some examples of the acceptable phrases are:

- Nurse Blank's personal appearance, or rather total lack of it, is surpassed only by his/her complete disregard for personal hygiene.

- The fact that not one trace of an acceptable personality can be found in Nurse Blank has not hindered his/her interrelations with other hospital personnel. (Nobody would talk to this ass-hole anyway!)

- It has been noted on several occasions that when Nurse Blank was faced with additional tasks, he/she cheerfully and enthusiastically leaped into total inactivity.

- It is my personal opinion that Nurse Blank is not worth a damn and that his/her departure from this assignment has brought a relief to the hospital that is akin only to that of a multiple orgasm.

- Nurse Blank performs all of his/her assigned tasks in a semi-adequate manner while constantly supervised.

- While assigned to this hospital, Nurse Blank displayed remarkable foresight and initiative and constantly strove to better himself/herself and the unit. However, the pure fact that this person was totally and helplessly inept and in all probability could not hit the damn ground with his hat should be mentioned.

- You will be fortunate to get Nurse Blank to work for you in any capacity.

Change to Nurses Policy and Procedures Manual

Subject: Nursing Staff Expectations

Management has long identified that the moral of individual nurses is enhanced by allowing them to select the shit that they want from a variety of options. While some nurses prefer the shorter daytime shit, others prefer to enjoy the longer twelve hour shit even though they only get three or four shits per week. Some nurses prefer a team approach, where select nurses participate in each shit and cheer each other on in the true spirit of camaraderie. Nothing can be more beneficial to the moral of the hospital as a group of nurses working together to provide the best possible shit.

Due to the extreme load and pressure, management is restricted to a standard shit so that they are available to provide additional shit to the nurses on a daily basis. It has been documented that managements shit and nurses shit do not mix well and certainly cannot be shared, so nurses should not expect management to give a shit.

Any changes in schedules must be documented and approved in advance. Remember that even if you feel that you have experienced a satisfactory shit, the job is not complete until the paperwork is finished.

(Please note that the letter "f " does not work on this typewriter.)

Change to Nurses Policy and Procedures Manual

The following outline has been developed to assist you in getting over the initial fear of public speaking. Merely highlight one of the choices and continue with your speech. Remember to stay within your time limits, as this will preclude your having to answer any difficult questions.

Good Morning, I am . . . .
- A) Your name
- B) Occupant
- C) Choosing to Remain Anonymous

I am . . .
- A) Honored to be
- B) Bored to Tears whenever I come
- C) Required to be
- D) Not really
. . . here.

I consider my time spent at this hospital . . . .
- A) Challenging
- B) A Reasonable Opportunity to chill out
- C) Punishment

During my stay here I intend to . . .
- A) Do my utmost
- B) Make a Reasonable Effort
- C) Appear to be doing a good job
- D) Keep a low profile

You can find me . . .
- A) In my office
- B) Out to lunch
- C) At happy hour
- D) At the Chaplains Office

In conclusion . . .
    A) Thank you very much for your welcome
    B) Who really cares?
    C) Where's the Beer and chips?

I appreciate your
    A) Attention
    B) Not asking any questions
    C) Snoring softly

If you need any assistance . . .
    A) I'll be glad to help
    B) See my assistant
    C) The Chaplains Office is down the street
    D) Here's a dime, call someone who cares!

Performance Evaluation Form

Employee Name: Date:
Title/Position:

Select the best description from each category

Knowledge:

A. This son of a bitch really knows her shit!
B. Knows just enough to be dangerous
C. Only have a brain and is dangerous
D. Bastard is brain damaged!

Attitude:

A. Extremely cooperative (if you kiss her ass!)
B. Brown noser
C. Often pisses off co-workers
D. Doesn't give a shit, never has, never will!

Reliability:

A. Really a dependable little shit
B. Can be relied on to be the first one out the door!
C. Totally worthless

Leadership:

A. Carries a chain saw and gets good results.
B. Better leader than Patton (at evaluation time)
C. Occasionally told by his subordinates to get screwed
D. Mother Theresa would tell this guy to go get screwed

Accuracy:

A. Does excellent work if not preoccupied with sex
B. Pretty good, seldom blows it out his ass
C. Has to take off his shoes to complete a blood count
D. Cannot count her tits and get the same number twice!

Appearance:

A. Extremely neat, even combs their pubic hair!
B. Looks great at evaluation time!
C. Dirty, filthy, smelly son of a bitch
D. Flies leave fresh dog shit to follow this person!

Performance:

A. Moves like a son of a bitch if there's money involved!
B. Works only if kicked in the ass every two minutes.
C. We feel this person died and failed to notify us.
D. Consistently manages to find new places to park.

At the College Entrance Exam students were asked to rearrange the following letters: **PNEIS**
The hint provided was that it was an important part of the human body that was most useful when erect.

- Some students rearranged the letters to read PENIS. They became doctors.
- Others rearranged the letters to read SPINE. They were sent to the Nursing School.

Doctor's Know Best . . . .

The nurse came rushing into the doctors office. She was very excited and explained to the doctor that the patient he had just given a clean bill of health to had walked into the waiting room and fainted. Another nurse ran in and explained that the patient was in the waiting room, but he had expired!

The doctor leapt to his feet and took action. He brushed past the nurses and into the waiting room. He called back to the nurses "Hurry up and help me! We have to turn this guy around so that it looks as if he was just coming in!"

The new nurse was being shown around the ward when a Doctor rushed past her, yelling. "Typhoid!" He blurted out. She saw him enter a patients room and exclaim "Tetanus!", then enter another room and yell out "Common Flu!"

She looked at her mentor and asked why the doctor was doing that. Her mentor looked at the doctor, then at the new nurse and explained.

"That's Doctor Edmonds. He just likes to call the shots around here. . ."

The young doctor had just finished his residency in Obstetrics and still felt uncomfortable when performed pelvic exams on some of his patients. As a method of relieving some of his anxiety he had picked up a habit of whistling softly while he worked.

When the middle aged woman began to chuckle, and then burst out laughing during her exam the doctor was even more embarrasses . . . and befuddled.

"I'm sorry," he told his patient. "Was I tickling you?"

"No", she replied. Tears were running down her face. The nurse leaned in to the doctor and made a recommendation.

"Perhaps a tune OTHER than 'I wish I were an Oscar Mayer Wiener' would be more appropriate . . ."

The new doctor entered the room where a woman and a baby were waiting. He glanced at the chart and examined the baby who seemed a little underweight. He turned to the woman and asked if the baby was bottle or breast fed.

"Breast fed" the woman replied.

"Please. Strip to your waist." The doctor ordered, and she complied. He pressed her breasts, kneaded and rubbed them both. Then he pinched her nipples in a very professional manner. Then he motioned for the woman to get dressed.

"No wonder this baby is underfed. You don't have any milk."

"I know." The woman admitted. "But you should know that his mother is down the hall with the nurse. I'm the child's grandmother. But I'm glad that I came in."

The young lady was admitted to the Emergency Room after an episode at a rock concert. Her gothic appearance was topped off with red and green hair trimmed into a Mohawk haircut. She had tattoos up and down her arm and wore leather buckles and studs.

She was quickly diagnosed with appendicitis and was scheduled for immediate surgery. Lying naked on the table the staff noticed that her pubic hair was also dyed a different color. It was green. And a tattoo above the hair read "Keep off the grass".

After completing the surgery the doctor checked the incisions and then paused. The staff watched him as he took out a marker and wrote a note on his patients dressing:

"Sorry . . . Had to mow the lawn . . ."

Miss Diagnosis

The patient came into the clinic and complained of passing out now and again. He said that when he passed out, he remembers hallucinations, but all the images were cartoon like. The nurse asked him to describe the images as she charted the patients vital information.

"Well, I saw Mickey Mouse on time. Another time I saw Donald Duck. Then, when I passed out at the wheel, I saw Goofy driving a car. One time I saw Chip and Dale. I don't understand what this all means."

The nurse thought for a moment, then wrote into the chart. She looked at the patient and told him not to worry.

"This happens quite often", she said. "You are just having Disney Spells."

One day I had to be the bearer of bad news when I told a wife that her husband had died of a massive myocardial infarct. Not more than five minutes later, I heard her reporting to the rest of the family that he had died of a "massive internal fart."

The Charge Nurse handed the new nurse the notes that she had done during Triage of a new patient.

"You have to work on your punctuation. This will confuse the doctor."

The nurse opened the chart and knew exactly what was meant. There, in her own penmanship was the patients complaint:

"Unable to eat diarrhea."

In Case Of Accident

While filling out an application for a job at a hospital, a nurse was puzzled by the blank after "Person to notify in case of accident". Finally she sighed and wrote, "Anybody in sight."

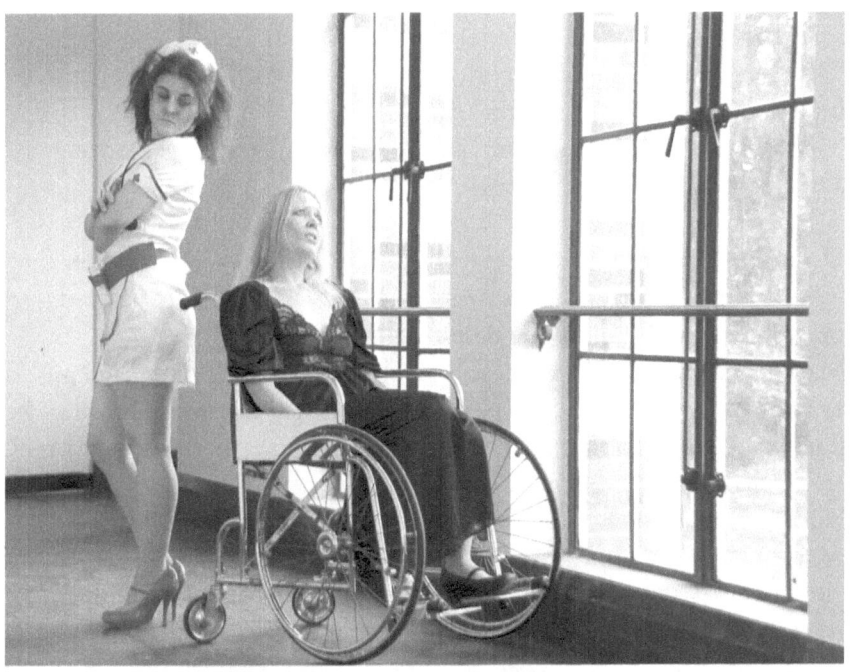

Nurses ensure that their patients are
cared for and get plenty of fresh air and sunlight.
(Model: Lindsay McCoy, Kendra Dicks)

Who's in charge?

During a visit to the mental asylum, I asked the Director how do you determine whether or not a patient should be institutionalized.

'Well,' said the Director, 'we fill up a bathtub, then we offer a teaspoon, a teacup and a bucket to the patient and ask him or her to empty the bathtub.'

'Oh, I understand,' I said. 'A normal person would use the bucket because it's bigger than the spoon or the teacup.'

'No.' said the Director, 'A normal person would pull the plug. Do you want a bed near the window?'

Jim and Mary were both patients in a Mental Hospital. One day while they were walking past the hospital swimming pool, Jim suddenly jumped into the deep end. He sunk to the bottom & stayed there.

Mary promptly jumped in to save him. She swam to the bottom and pulled Jim out. When the medical director became aware of Mary's heroic act he immediately ordered her to be discharged from the hospital, as he now considered her to be mentally stable.

When he went to tell Mary the news he said, "Mary, I have good news & bad news. The good news is you're being discharged because since you were able to jump in and save the life of another patient, I think you've regained your senses." The bad news is, Jim, the patient you saved, hung himself with his bathrobe belt in the bathroom. I am so sorry, but he's dead."

Mary replied "He didn't hang himself . . . I put him there to dry."

Arriving at the Emergency Room with an inflamed appendix, the motorcycle patrolman was rushed into surgery. He felt relieved when the drugs kicked in and the pain subsided, then he passed out. The last thing he heard was a masked person assuring him that everything would be just fine. When he woke in the ward the patrolman felt something pulling on the hairs of his chest. It hurt and he wondered what went wrong in surgery. After mustering his energy he was able to look at his chest and see what was causing the discomfort.

Taped firmly and securely across his very hairy chest were several strips of heavy duty adhesive tape. He tugged at them but they didn't easily move, only pulled at the hairs on his chest. Written in large black letters across the tape were some words from one of the ER staff:

"Get well quickly. From the nurse that you gave a ticket to last Monday . . ."

The new nurse arrived at the Emergency Room and was chatting in the hall with the ER doctor. The rest of the staff gathered at the Nurses Station to size up the newest member of the family. And she was a knockout! She had been a volunteer cheerleader for the local NFL for two years and even in the baggy scrubs that everyone wore, her figure was stunning.

The doctor stood in the hallway with her, chatting about just about anything. They continued to chat as the staff went about their normal routine. Every time they came back to the Nurses Station, they glanced at the new nurse and the doctor in the hallway. It was a scene out of high school!

"We need to get the doctor back on his rounds." Nurse Teasdale mentioned, and started to head towards the couple.

"No, no!" The Charge Nurse interjected! "We have a pool going! We want to see how long Doctor Meaks can hold his stomach in!"

You are going to die . . .

A husband and wife went to the doctor together. The doctor called the husband into the room to examine him. After examining him, he called in the wife. He said I'm afraid I have some bad news. Your husband is suffering from a very rare disease. In order for him to live, you would have to do everything for him such as, wait on him hand foot. You would have to run his bath water, get the news paper for him to read, basically answer to all of his beaconed calls, if not he will die. The doctor stated, this will only last for one year.
As they were leaving the doctor's office, the husband asked his wife, so what did the doctor tell you? She informed him "The Doctor said you are going to die!!!"

The nervous patient confided in the nurse. "I'm terribly worried about coming to the hospital. Just last week I read in the newspaper about a woman who came to the hospital for heart trouble and died from meningitis. I'm really concerned."
The nurse didn't miss a beat. "Ma'am", she said.
"This is the best hospital in the state, so relax. When we treat someone for heart trouble, they die of heart trouble . . ."

The patient finally got some time to speak privately with the Nurse. He was a big burly man and it was obviously difficult for him to broach the subject. "I have to tell you this. It's embarrassing, but every time I have sex, I cry. Is that normal?"
"Well, not normally." The Nurse replied. "But then again, this is a Federal Prison."

A Nurse at Heaven

Three nurses died & went to heaven where they were met at the Pearly Gates by St. Peter. Saint Peter asks the first nurse, "What did you do on Earth that would earn you a spot in heaven?"

"I was a nurse in an inner city hospital," she replied. "I worked to bring healing and peace to the poor suffering city children."

"Very noble," said St. Peter. "You may enter." And in through the gates she went.

He asks the second nurse the same question, "So what did you do on Earth?"

"I was a nurse at a missionary hospital in Africa," she replied. "For many years, I worked with a skeleton crew of doctors and nurses who tried to reach out to as many peoples and tribes with a hand of healing and with a message of God's love."

"How touching," said St. Peter. "You too may enter." And in she went.

Then Saint Peter turned to the last nurse.

"What did you do back on Earth?"

After some hesitation, she explained, "I was just a nurse at an H.M.O."

St. Peter pondered this for a moment and then looked at her.

"Okay, you may also enter."

"Whew!" said the nurse. "For a moment there, I thought you weren't going to let me in."

"Oh, you can come in," said St. Peter, "but you can only stay for three days . . ."

A nurse dies and goes to heaven. She is met at the Pearly Gates by St. Peter who asks her questions about her life. Over St. Peter's shoulder the nurse spots a man in a white coat sitting on a cloud with a stethoscope around his neck. "Oh brother!", she cries. "Is that a doctor?" St Peter glances over his shoulder and says, "No, that's God. He just thinks he's a doctor."

What's the difference between a nurse and a nun? A nun only serves one God.

Nursing Homes

One evening a family brings their frail, elderly mother to a nursing home and leaves her as planned, hoping she will be well cared for.

The next morning, the nurses bathe her, feed her a tasty breakfast, and set her in a chair at a window overlooking a lovely flower garden.

She seems OK, but after a while she slowly starts to lean over sideways in her chair. Two attentive nurses immediately rush up to catch her and straighten her up. Again she seems OK, but after a while she starts to tilt to the other side. The nurses rush back and once more bring her back upright. This goes on all morning. Later the family arrives to see how the old woman is adjusting to her new home. "So Ma, how is it here? Are they treating you all right?" they ask.

"It's pretty nice," she replies. "Except . . . they won't let me fart."

The patient was tossing and turning all night. In the morning, the nurse came in and noticed that he had been chewing on the pillow throughout the night. She asked the patient how he felt.

"I'm O.K. Just a little down in the mouth . . ."

The nurse was completing the check in form for her elderly patient and asked "How long have you been bedridden."

The patient thought for a moment. Then she replied, "Well, I guess for about fifteen years now . . . when my husband was alive."

While visiting my 85 year old grandfather in the hospital I asked him how he was feeling.

"Feeling just fine, thanks for asking." "Is the food ok here?" I asked. "Terrific food. Couldn't be better." He assured me.

"How about the nursing care. Do they treat you all right?"

"Top notch! Great group of young nurses out there."

"Are you sleeping all right?" I ask.

"Like a baby. Nine hours of solid sleep every night. At ten pm they bring me a nice hot cup of hot chocolate and a Viagra pill. I take the pill and wash it down with the hot chocolate and I'm gone for the night." He tells me.

I was puzzled as to why they were giving grandpa Viagra at night. At the end of the visit I stopped by the nurses station and asked the nurse in charge about it.

"Oh, that." She says. "Yes, on nightly rounds we started a dose of Viagra and hot chocolate for your grandfather to help him sleep at night. The chocolate makes him sleepy and the Viagra keeps him from rolling out of bed."

Whenever things got really hectic at the Nurses Station, the Charge Nurse would take a deep breathe and pull a photograph of her husband out of her purse. After gazing at his face for a few moments, she would get back to work with a new zeal.

After watching this routine for several months, one of the doctors commented on her ritual, adding "He must be quite an inspiration to you"

"Yes, he is, doctor. No matter how crazy things get here at work, I am comforted by knowing that if I can survive being married to that psycho, I can survive anything!"

Thermometers:

What's the difference between an oral thermometer and a rectal thermometer?
The taste.

Exhausted after a twelve hour shift, Nurse Noreen stops by the Denny's for coffee on her way home. The waitress drops off the check and Noreen gets ready to sign the bill.
At the counter she pulls a rectal thermometer out of her pocket. The waitress stares at the thermometer. Noreen looks up at the waitress. Without missing a beat, she says, "Perfect! Some asshole has my pen!"

Why do senior nurses insist on using the rectal thermometer to obtain temperatures?
They have learned to always look for the patients best side.

Miss Communication

During a patient's two week follow-up appointment with his cardiologist, he informed his doctor that he was having trouble with one of his medications. "Which one?" asked the doctor. "The patch." The nurse told me to put on a new one every six hours and now I'm running out of places to put it!"
The doctor had him quickly undress and discovered what he hoped he wouldn't see . . . . Yes, the man had over fifty patches on his body! Now the instructions include removal of the old patch before applying a new one.

A man comes into the ER and yells, "My wife's going to have her baby in the cab!" The ER physician grabs his stuff, rushes out to the cab, lifts the lady's dress, and begins to take off her underwear. Suddenly he notices that there are several cabs, and he's in the wrong one!

The doctor stood in front of his patient as he listened to her lungs with his stethoscope. "Big breaths" he told his elderly patient.
"They used to be" replied the woman.

The Nurse Manager had posted a notice in the nurses break room for all to see.
"Remember . . . The first five minutes of a human beings live are the most dangerous . . ." The notice read. Beneath it someone has scrawled:
"The last five are pretty risky, too!"

The patient was to be discharged in the afternoon and the Nurse took a wheel chair to the room as required by hospital policy. There she me an elderly man who was dressed and sitting on the bed with a suitcase on the ground in front of him. The nurse explained that all patients must be wheeled out of the hospital using the wheel chair provided. He insisted that he didn't need any help leaving the hospital and the Nurse explained that 'rules are rules' . . .
Reluctantly he got into the wheelchair and was wheeled onto the elevator. The nurse cheerily asked him if his wife was going to meet him. "I really don't know." The man replied. "She's still upstairs in the bathroom changing out of her hospital gown."

In the break room the cute young nurse confided to the resident psychiatrist over a cup of coffee.

"I don't know what to do, Doctor. Every time I get friendly with one of the young doctors here I end up dating him. Then we end up at my place and things get, well. You know . . . frisky. Then I feel guilty and depressed for a week."

The older doctor nodded his head. "I see. And you want me to do something to help you strengthen your will power so that you don't get into these entanglements, don't you?"

"Hell no!" exclaimed the pretty nurse. "I want you to fix it so that I don't feel guilty and depressed afterward!"

The doctor was checking on his patients in the hospital. He asked how the food was and the patient only had one complaint.

"It's that Kentucky Jelly. First off, it's hard to open, and I just can't get used to the taste of it."

The doctor surveyed the breakfast tray, nodded and made a note of it. He assured his patient that he'd take care of it. On his way by the nurses station he informed the staff not to give his patient any more of the Kentucky Jelly. They looked at him with questioning eyes. Then he held up the foil packet for them to see. It was clearly labeled. "KY Jelly".

Suzie was working the Telenurse station and was absolutely amazed at some of the conversations she had with some of the callers. For example:

Suzie: "Mercy Hospital Telenurse, my name is Suzie. How can I help you?"

Caller: "I need a ride to the hospital."

Suzie: "I can arrange that for you. I need some information. What is your name and where are you?"

Caller: "I'm in another hospital. Can you get me out of here? Transfer me to your hospital?"

Suzie: "OK, we'll have to get a transfer from your doctor. What is his name?"

Caller: "No, don't call him. You'll just get me in trouble. I just need a ride to your hospital."

Suzie: "Well, we have to tell the staff there about…"

Caller: "No! You can't! Don't tell them a thing. They hate me here. The doctors are incompetent. I just need a ride to your hospital. Can you get me a limousine?"

Suzie: "A limousine? I don't think so. An ambulance is usually called for these transfers."

Caller: "I want a limousine. A black one. With a nurse in the back to help me during the trip. Can you do that?"

Suzie: (Checking the caller ID-) "I see that you are in the Holy Oaks Sanitarium. It that the correct location?"

Caller: "Yeah, can you get me out of here?"

Suzie: "How about if I send a nice limousine with two student nurses to help you. They will cater to your every whim. When you get here, it'll be lunch time and we can have them wheel you to the cafeteria, where we have a stringed quartet playing music for the patients. And the nurses give massages at three."

Caller: "Massages? String Quartet? Are you sure? That just sounds… well…I'd be crazy to believe you would do that for me!"

Suzie: "And that's why you are at Holy Oak Asylum… Goodbye…"

www.ingramcontent.com/pod-product-compliance
Lightning Source LLC
Chambersburg PA
CBHW021050180526
45163CB00005B/2360